RENO AIR RACING

Michael O'Leary

Motorbooks International
Publishers & Wholesalers ®

First published in 1996 by Motorbooks International
Publishers & Wholesalers, 729 Prospect Avenue, PO
Box 1, Osceola, WI
54020-0001 USA

Motorbooks International is a certified trademark,
registered with the United States Patent Office

The information in this book is true and complete to
the best of our knowledge. All recommendations are
made without any guarantee on the part of the
author or Publisher, who also disclaim any liability
incurred in connection with the use of this data or
specific details

We recognize that some words, model names and
designations, for example, mentioned herein are the
property of the trademark holder. We use them for
identification purposes only. This is not an official
publication

Motorbooks International books are also available at
discounts in bulk quantity for industrial or sales-
promotional use. For details write to Special Sales
Manager at the Publisher's address

Library of Congress Cataloging-in-Publication Data

O' Leary, Michael
    Reno air racing / Michael O'Leary.
        p. cm. -- (Enthusiasts color series)
    Includes index.
    ISBN 0-7603-0084-4 (pbk. : alk. paper)
    1. Airplane racing--Nevada--Reno. 2.
Airplanes, Racing.
    I. Title. II. Series.
    GV759.044 1996
    797.5'2--dc20   96-13069

On the front cover: Pilot Alan Preston is flying *Dago
Red* on a test flight while accompanied by Bruce
Lockwood in *Miss America*.

On the frontispiece: This frontal view of Lyle Shelton's
Rare Bear emphasizes its drastically reduced
wingspan.

On the title page: An interesting contrast in Unlimited-
air-racing history. At the 1994 Phoenix 500, we were
able to pose *Rare Bear* with Delmar Benjamin's
magnificent Gee Bee R-2 replica racer (see the
Enthusiast Color Series book *Gee Bee*, by Delmar
Benjamin and Steve Wolf for the complete story on
building and flying this replica Golden Age air racer).
At Reno 1994, John Penney would win the much-
maligned Super Gold race (which pitted the three
fastest, or at least the three fastest *surviving* racers) at a
slow speed of 424.407 miles per hour (after qualifying
at 471.325 miles per hour).

On the back cover: *Strega* has one of the best
prepared crews at Reno. The racer is seen
undergoing maintenance under the protection of its
red tent.

Printed in Hong Kong

Contents

Introduction

Before and after World War II, Cleveland, Ohio, was the site of the National Air Races. Very well attended by the general public, these races were at the forefront of aviation development during the 1920s and 1930s.

Cleveland saw participation by both military and civilian racing craft. Military officials were in for a rude shock as their latest pursuit aircraft were outstripped in performance by hot civilian racers—aircraft often built in a garage or in the back of a hangar by very talented, and often self-taught individuals who had a burning desire to advance the science of American aeronautics.

Many of these "homebuilt" advances were incorporated into the new generation of American warplanes—aircraft that would soon see combat as America entered the arena of World War II.

After the conclusion of World War II, the Cleveland National Air Races resumed, but the field was now dominated by surplus ex-military fighters—Airacobras, Mustangs, Lightnings, Kingcobras, etc. The day of the backyard racer was over and the unlimited racing class was now the domain of the planes that had won the war.

The Cleveland races lasted until 1950. Beset with problems such as accidents, urban encroachment, and the Korean War, the famous racing venue took down its pylons forever.

However, in 1964 unlimited air racing made a return. Promoter and pilot Bill Stead felt that there was a market for once again seeing those colorful, powerful, and historic aircraft battle it out around the pylons—and he was right. The Reno National Air Races, held annually every September, have gone on to become the world's longest running aviation competition event.

In this volume we present a look at some of these unlimited racing aircraft—mainly from the present but with a few golden oldies thrown in for good measure. These aircraft have carried on with the evolution of speed around the Reno pylons (and also other racing venues such as Mojave and Phoenix). Some of these aircraft, such as Lyle Shelton's *Rare Bear*, could fill an entire volume this size by themselves.

Unlimited air racing is an extremely expensive proposition, and the racers—now today's revered Warbirds—have become very valuable. As this book goes to press, we are seeing a modest return to "homebuilt" unlimited air racers (although the term homebuilt is relative since a great deal of expertise and technology is going into them) as the last major goal of unlimited pylon air racing—a 500 mph lap speed—comes closer and closer to reality.

Michael O'Leary
Los Angeles, California

David Price and *Dago Red* prepare to do battle with John Penney and *Rare Bear* at Reno 1995. After *Dago Red*'s 1982 debut, Destefani sold his interest to Frank Taylor. In 1983, Taylor took *Dago* over a 15-kilometer course to set a new record of 517.02 miles per hour, beating Jacqueline Cochran's 1951 P-51C record by 51 miles per hour.

CHAPTER ONE

Mustang Magnificence

*Arguably the greatest
all-around fighter aircraft of World War II, the North American P-51 Mustang is the most
numerous, and in many racing circles the most desirable,
of all Unlimited air racers.*

The history of the North American P-51 Mustang as a racing aircraft could fill up several large volumes. However, by way of a brief introduction, the Mustang came into being in a rather unusual manner. During the late 1930s, the free nations of Europe were in a panic trying to modernize their military forces to cope with the threat presented by the Nazis. The fledgling company North American Aviation, located in Inglewood, California, had established a good reputation for building sturdy training aircraft.

A British aircraft purchasing commission approached the company in 1940 with a proposal to build Curtiss P-40 fighters under license. However, North American considered the P-40 to be an obsolete and inferior fighting machine and brashly told the Brits that the company could build the Royal Air Force a much superior fighter.

The Brits put a rather unreasonable demand that the new plane had to be ready in just 120 days. The US government decided

The fastest and most successful of all Unlimited Mustangs, *Strega* started out life as a P-51D, USAAF serial number (s/n) 44-13105, which was transferred to the Royal Australian Air Force as A68-679 in July 1945. After being surplused in December 1948, the aircraft went through several owners, finally winding up in a small Australian aviation museum. In 1980, the plane was purchased by Dave Zeuschel and then sold to Destefani to become the basis for his new racing mount. Destefani decided to build his new racer in the style of *Dago Red* but to incorporate a number of changes, including a canopy design borrowed from the *Red Baron*, which allowed the canopy to be opened in flight—a real safety plus. The vertical fin was repositioned one-half degree to the right, while the engine and oil cooling system is basically the same as on *Dago Red*. When Destafani completed his new racer, registered N71FT, race number 7, the plane weighed in empty at 6,275 pounds, just 25 pounds heavier than *Dago*. First introduced at Reno 1983 and piloted by Ron Hevle, the new racer qualified third at 436 miles per hour. Hevle had to drop out of the Gold race after less than one lap, with mechanical problems. In this unusual formation photograph, *Strega* is accompanied by Delmar Benjamin in his Gee Bee R-2—both aircraft carrying race number 7 identification, but a world of aerodynamic differences separate the two classics.

Tiger Destefani had obtained the sponsorship of Skoal Tobacco and decided to pilot the aircraft himself at Reno 1985. However, various problems plagued the racer, and Destefani qualified at seventh and did not get into the Gold. Aerodynamically the cleanest of all current racing Mustangs, *Strega* came in third at Reno 1986 at 416.879 miles per hour, but by Reno 1987, *Strega* was really moving—taking the Gold at 452.559 miles per hour.

to let the British move ahead but with the condition that two of the first aircraft be given to the US Army Air Corps. North American made the deadline with the NA-73X (the company designation), powered by an Allison V-1710, and free-lance test pilot Vance Breese took the fighter aloft on 26 October 1940.

The British gave the plane the name "Mustang" and placed an initial order for 320 of the fighters, which featured the new and advanced laminar-flow wing. The Allison was

The most modified of all Mustang racers, *Stiletto* is seen in its ultimate racing form on 28 August 1992 with Matt Jackson at the controls. Nineteen ninety-two was the last racing season for race number 84, which at this point had been modified with a unique radiator boil-off system, thus eliminating the wing openings for the earlier wing-installed radiators. The boil-off system is working perfectly in this photograph, and steam can be seen pumping from the outlet immediately ahead of the pilot. The radiators were located in a special tank ahead of the pilot and immersed in liquid for cooling, thus eliminating all openings except for the extreme nose scoop—making *Stiletto* the most streamlined of all Mustang racers. Race number 84, N332, was conceived by Alan Preston during the early 1980s to be the fastest of all pylon racers. Accordingly, Preston contracted with Dave Zeuschel, who assembled a talented crew to create the new racing machine. Basically built out of parts from discarded airframes, *Stiletto* was radical in the fact that it originally was built to have its radiators located in the wing, thus eliminating the belly scoop. From the start of the project, every effort was made to reduce weight, and every nonracing part was discarded, while some were remanufactured from magnesium. Even the starter was eliminated, thus the aircraft had to rely on a ground power unit for start-up.

Stiletto in flight during April 1986 with Skip Holm at the controls. This view shows the clean under surface of the craft and also the short wing—just 28 feet, 11 inches in span. Modified P-51H radiators were installed in the wing with two elements of the H radiators in the left wing for coolant while the right wing had one unit with the aftercooler radiator. Heated air from the radiators was dispersed through wing slots. Among the many modifications, the pilot's position was moved 20 inches aft. *Stiletto* was fitted with 110-gallon bladder fuel tanks in the wing fuel bays and a smaller 25-gallon fuel tank located outboard of the aftercooler radiator. Zeuschel's weight-reduction program paid off for, when completed, *Stiletto* weighed just 5,800 pounds empty, the lightest of all Mustang racers. *Stiletto* caused a sensation when it showed up at Reno 1984, and Skip Holm immediately set a new Gold-race record at 437.62 miles per hour. For the 1985 and 1986 racing season, Preston obtained sponsorship from Color Tile Inc., and the racer carried their logo.

Scott Sherman is seen flying *Stiletto* near Cape Canaveral, Florida, during March 1989. At this point, the aircraft featured a revised paint scheme and a second seat behind the pilot for any individual brave or foolhardy enough to fly in the most radical of racing machines. *Stiletto* never achieved its full potential and dropped out of its last Reno event during 1992 with mechanical problems. As this is being written, *Stiletto* is in the final stages of modification—being converted to a stock dual-control TF-51D for the Museum of Flying.

basically a low-level engine, and the early Mustangs were great down low but quickly ran out of power as they gained altitude to do battle with the Luftwaffe. In 1942, Rolls-Royce received five of the early Mustangs for experimental fitting of Merlin powerplants. The combination of the Merlin with the Mustang was magic (although it took North American engineers to create the amazing belly air scoop for the radiator that actually helped increase the P-51's top speed). The new Merlin-powered machine was designated the P-51B, and orders poured in. When the Mustang was later fitted with a bubble

One of the most competitive, and most attractive, racing Mustangs is *Dago Red*, which is currently owned by David Price's Museum of Flying. With Price at the controls, *Dago Red* had one of its best racing seasons ever during Reno 1995 when it qualified at 458.182 miles per hour and finished the Gold race in third place at 449.137. In this view, taken on 8 September 1994, Alan Preston is flying *Dago Red* on a test flight above Mojave, California, while accompanied by Bruce Lockwood in *Miss America*.

canopy, it became the P-51D, and the type became the best all-around fighter of World War II, and over 14,000 examples were built.

When the Cleveland National Air Races began after World War II, the Mustang was a sought-after machine, but Merlin-powered examples were not that easy to come by, since the type was still being extensively used by the US Army Air Forces (USAAF) and was also being supplied to the air forces of many of America's allies. Early Allison-powered Mustangs distinguished themselves around the pylons, but as soon as the Merlin-powered aircraft became available in surplus sales, they took over. However, even the Merlin-powered Mustangs still faced stiff competition from the F2G Super Corsairs. In the

This is what racing looks like from above—Alan Preston and Bruce Lockwood are seen going low and fast around the practice course at Mojave. *Dago Red* started life as a damaged Mustang airframe, N5410V, purchased by Tiger Destefani and Frank Taylor in 1980 with the goal of making a highly modified pylon racer.

A unique view of Alan Preston in *Dago Red* and David Price in *Cottonmouth* as the two racers fly formation with the F/A-18 Hornets of the Blue Angels on 28 February 1992. Considered, by modern standards, to be a "small" fighter, the Hornet dwarfs the Mustang. *Dago Red* was unleashed on Reno in 1982 and with pilot Ron Hevle qualified first at 440 miles per hour and then won the Gold race at 405 miles per hour—an excellent debut.

cross-country Bendix Race, Mustangs dominated the field.

In 1964, the Reno National Air Races started, and Mustangs were the most numerous aircraft to compete. However, the sleek North Americans faced lots of competition over the years from Bearcats, modified Sea Furys, and the Super Corsair as well as a new generation of specifically built Unlimiteds. Some experts stated that the day of the Mustang was over, that the Merlin did not develop enough horsepower and was too unreliable as a highly modified powerplant, but the Mustang has fought back and speeds have increased dramatically. It is fitting that, as this book goes to press, Bill "Tiger" Destefani in his highly modified P-51D *Strega* was the champion of Reno 1995 —beating out his archrival, the F8F *Rare Bear*. There's still lots of life in North American's most famous thoroughbred!

Bruce Lockwood flies a tight formation with *Dago* while a stock Mustang offers an excellent comparison with the racer. By late 1985, *Dago* had passed into the ownership of Alan Preston, who was able to field two of the fastest Unlimiteds—*Dago* and *Stiletto*. At Reno 1986, Preston set a new record by entering an aircraft in each of the four racing classes (Formula One, Biplane, Texan, and Unlimited) and flew *Dago* to fourth place in the Gold at 413 miles per hour.

In 1983, Rick Brickert took over the piloting duties of *Dago*, qualifying the plane at Reno at 439 miles per hour but being knocked out of the Gold race with a broken spinner. In 1984, Brickert had *Dago* at full power in the Gold when the Merlin came apart. Merlins are famed for not catching fire after failing, but this time a broken rod caused an engine fire. Brickert pulled up with a Mayday and rolled the canopy back (which immediately departed the aircraft). Fire entered the cockpit but Rick got the plane safely on the ground without injuries. Somebody found the shattered canopy in the desert and returned it to Brickert who is seen holding part of it aloft with a very singed *Dago* in the background.

Arguably one of the most attractive of all Mustang Unlimiteds, the late Dave Zeuschel is seen flying race number 69 *Jeannie* on a test flight (note tufted belly scoop) shortly before Reno 1981. NX79111 has a long history of air racing, including participation at the postwar Thompson Trophy races, and during the 1970s and 1980s *Jeannie* was developed by Zeuschel as one of the most potent of all racing Unlimiteds. For owner Wiley Sanders, Zeuschel undertook an extensive lightening program on the racer, getting weight down to 6,100 pounds. The exploits of this aircraft could fill a book, but one of the most epic occurred on 5 September 1980. The aircraft had been groomed for Reno, and Zeuschel was taking off from Van Nuys Airport for one last test flight. Without warning, the engine quit and Dave had no choice but to find a landing spot. With gear up and low on speed, he glided over a model-airplane flying field (setting the modelers scattering) and bellied the plane into a cornfield, tearing off the propeller, belly scoop, and doing considerable damage to the airframe. It looked as if race number 69's racing career was over for at least a couple of years. However, owner Wiley Sanders decided to pump money into the plane, so Zeuschel assembled the most talented team in air-racing history and had the damaged plane up and flying in just four days. Reno officials had heard about the accident and scrubbed *Jeannie* from the racing list, so they were amazed to see pilot Mac MacClain set the patched-up racer down on the Reno runway just a half-hour before the final entrance deadline. That the racer got to Reno was amazing enough, but MacClain battled through qualifications and heat races to win the Gold Championship Race at 433 miles per hour—a new Reno record. For Reno 1981, rookie Skip Holm qualified *Jeannie* at 450.085—another Reno record—and won the Gold at 431 miles per hour. Today, the aircraft is in storage in Florida.

One of the most famous of all racing aircraft is P-51D *Miss America*. One of the longest-running competitors at Reno, race number 11 has had several owners and numerous modifications. At Reno 1994, Alan Preston flew the aircraft for owner Brent Hisey and won the Gold race, beating out the much more competitive *Dago Red* flown by David Price. At Reno 1995, Hisey took over the controls and qualified at 346.377 miles per hour, coming in second in the Bronze race at 349.918 miles per hour.

NEXT PAGES
Robert Converse's P-51D N471R, race number 71, is an excellent example of a cleaned-up Mustang airframe with some racing modifications (including clipped wing tips) that makes for a competitive Unlimited. At Reno 1995, Converse qualified *Huntress III* at 347.377 miles per hour and finished fifth in the Bronze race at 307.870 miles per hour.

Bill Rheinschild has proven to be a top competitor in his P-51D, race number 45, *Risky Business*. Over the years, the aircraft has received numerous modifications to help increase top speeds. N34FF is seen during an October 1988 test flight with Matt Jackson at the controls.

One of the wildest of all highly modified Mustang Unlimiteds was Tom Kelly's race number 19, *Vendetta*, which made its initial appearance at Reno 1988 with John Dilley at the controls. The plane mated a highly modified P-51D fuselage with the wing and horizontal tail of a Learjet to create one of the most attractive racing aircraft of all time. Unfortunately, engine problems kept *Vendetta* out of the running, and the plane was heavily damaged in a forced landing the following year. However, racers have a Phoenix-like quality, and *Vendetta* was being rebuilt for racing as this book went to press.

Every year, Reno sees a good turnout of stock Mustangs that are pulled around the pylons just for the hell of it. Two such machines are seen at Reno 1993.

Another highly modified and extremely competitive Mustang is race number 69, *Georgia Mae*, owned by Wiley Sanders and flown in this July 1990 photograph by John Putnam. The aircraft had been virtually destroyed in a landing accident at an earlier Reno but was completely rebuilt by Sanders. Sanders became discouraged with air racing, however, and by 1990 had withdrawn both of his Mustang racers from further participation.

Another extremely attractive and competitive Unlimited is John Crocker's race number 6, *Sumthin Else*. Designed and built by Jim Larsen, the aircraft was highly competitive in Reno Gold races but was damaged in a landing accident at a 1990 airshow and has remained in storage since. A respected airline, warbird, and race pilot, John Crocker was killed in the crash of a Convair C-131 in February 1996.

RIGHT

Wildly painted race number 55, *Voodoo Chile*, with rookie Bob "Buckwheat" Hannah heads out for the start of the Reno 1995 Gold race. Hannah qualified the plane at an impressive 440.080 miles per hour and finished the Gold in fifth place with a very sick Merlin at 405.925 miles per hour.

PILOT: Hurricane Bob Hannah

Voodoo Chile

The racer that never was. For a period of time, Joe Kasparoff owned three Mustangs including this rare P-51B, which had been restored by Pete Regina and raced once in the Bronze event by Skip Holm. After Kasparoff acquired the plane, he finished it in this magnificent racing scheme but never entered the craft at Reno. The plane is seen during a maintenance flight on 21 June 1993, being piloted by Matt Jackson.

The late and great *Red Baron*. Owned by Ed Browning, P-51D N7715C, race number 5, had been heavily modified and fitted with a Dave Zeuschel-built Rolls Royce Griffon V-12 with contra-rotating propellers. The Griffon was built for use in later-model Spitfires and is a 2,239-cubic-inch powerplant capable of a stock horsepower rating of 2,500 horsepower at 2,750 rpm. Zeuschel and Browning worked closely to develop the *Red Baron* as the world's fastest racing plane, and it became just that. On 14 August 1979, Steve Hinton took the *Red Baron* out over a measured course at Tonopah, Nevada, to set a new absolute speed record of 499.059 miles per hour—thus taking the 10-year-old record away from Darryl Greenamyer. However, at the September Reno event, the big Griffon came apart during the Gold race, and the plane crashed. Hinton amazingly survived the crash but was badly injured. Fortunately, Steve recovered and went on to race at Reno once again.

RIGHT
The start of the 1988 Reno Gold race was marred by a sudden Mayday call from Don Whittington in race number 09. A weld had failed, pumping oil out of the complex propeller mechanism and sending the six prop blades into flat pitch—something akin to hanging an anchor from the sleek racer. Don pulled off a skilled belly landing but, as can be seen, the beautiful Unlimited would need lots of repair work.

LEFT
Race pilot and warbird collector Don Whittington was fascinated by the big Griffon V-12, and he built up a highly modified Mustang to handle the powerplant. A lighter racer than the *Red Baron*, race number 09, *Precious Metal*, made its racing debut at Reno 1988 where Whittington qualified the aircraft at 453.5 miles per hour.

By Reno 1995, race number 38 was further modified to sport the larger vertical tail from a P-51H. Whittington qualified the racer at 380.317 miles per hour and had several mechanical problems hamper his top speed. He went on to win the Silver race at 379.491 miles per hour but elected to forfeit his win in order to compete in the Gold. In that event, the beautifully polished aluminum and bright green racer finished in sixth position at 390.456 miles per hour.

John Penney in *Rare Bear* heads out for the Gold event at the 1994 Phoenix 500—which he won handily at an average speed of 434.158. On the first lap, he was following Alan Preston in *Dago Red* when Preston cut the hard-to-see pylon number 6, and Penney followed him. However, by the end of the race, John was far enough ahead to overcome the cut and maintain his position in first. With some help from his on-board nitrous oxide bottles, Penney was hitting the first few laps in the 460s but began throttling back as he increased *Rare Bear*'s lead.

CHAPTER TWO

Cat with Claws

The US Navy's last propeller-driven fighter was designed, in part, to combat World War II's Japanese kamikaze threat. Today, it is the most potent of all Unlimited racing aircraft.

It is a paradox that one of today's most highly-prized warbird fighters is also the holder of the majority of Unlimited racing records. The paradox occurs because of the fact that many warbird owners are purists, restoring their valuable aircraft down to the finest detailing of the smallest original components, while the Unlimited racing fraternity takes the same aircraft, strips out all original military equipment, changes the engine and propeller, adds a low-profile canopy, and performs many other changes that are all guaranteed to drive the purist warbirder right up the hangar wall. (Expect to pay well over $1 million if, and when, you can find a Bearcat for sale).

The Grumman F8F Bearcat is one of our rarest surviving propeller-driven fighters that was designed during World War II. As of this writing, only about eight are flyable but several other airframes are under restoration.

Beginning with the FF-1 two-seat biplane fighter, Grumman established itself as the major supplier of fighter aircraft to the US Navy. During the 1930s, the company progressed through the F2F and F3F biplanes—perhaps the penultimate American combat biplanes—to the dawn of the monoplane fighter age. Grumman's next design, XF4F-1, started out life as a biplane, but the design was quickly changed to the XF4F-2 monoplane in

Bearcat power at its best: Pilot Jack Sliker runs up the mighty Pratt & Whitney R-2800 radial while the white-painted Skyraider propeller contrasts in size to the clipped wing span. Surplused in 1963, F8F-2 BuNo 122708, N7701C, was one of the few Bearcats to survive the final scrappings at Naval Air Station Litchfield Park, Arizona, before that facility was closed and military aircraft storage was consolidated at Davis-Monthan Air Force Base. If there had been more civilian interest in the powerful fighter, more F8Fs would have survived since they were being sold to anyone who wanted the planes, but the majority of the final batch of stored F8Fs was simply fed into the furnace. In 1973, N7701C was purchased by Sliker of Wadley, Georgia. Sliker already owned a P-51D he used for air racing, and he had similar plans for the more powerful 'Cat. Besides the clipped outer wing panels, other modifications include removal of the rollover structure and addition of a spinner. Photographed at the 1975 Mojave Air Races held in June, Sliker went on to attend the September Reno event, where he finished third in the Gold race at 381.97 miles per hour. While returning home on 16 September, Sliker apparently ran the craft out of fuel while on final approach to the airport at Flagstaff, Arizona, and was killed in the resulting crash.

order to keep up with the rapidly changing combat standards that were being defined and redefined by the European nations. However, Grumman's F4F design lost out to another plane, the Brewster F2A Buffalo.

Even though Brewster won the battle, it did not win the war. The US Navy decided to hedge its bet and placed an order with Grumman for an improved Wildcat. From 7 December 1941, the Buffalo proved to be a death trap for Navy and Marine pilots and was rapidly withdrawn from the combat role,

Looking every bit the potent racing machine it could be, F8F-2P BuNo 121787, N148F, is seen at Mojave, California, during October 1973 at one of the several Unlimited air races held at the remote ex-Marine Corps airfield. Starting civil life as N6821D in 1963, the 'Cat was obtained by Bud Fountain's Hawke Dusters, based at Modesto, California, and several modifications were made for racing. The anodized-aluminum finish that Grumman carefully gave each of its Bearcats to prevent salt-water corrosion was sanded off by Fountain's crew, and the raw aluminum underneath was highly polished. During the unlimited race on 20 October, the Pratt & Whitney R-2800 radial let go, and an intense fire started, fed by the engine's magnesium parts. The Bearcat does not have much in the way of a firewall, so the flames almost immediately entered the cockpit. The Bearcat fell as a fire ball onto the desert floor, exploding on impact in front of the thousands of spectators.

Before the appearance of *Rare Bear*, the F8F most associated with air racing was the Bearcat flown so skillfully and victoriously by Lockheed test pilot Darryl Greenamyer. Greenamyer actually won the first Reno event but was disqualified when he decided not to land on the terrible dirt runway (fearing that the craft's high-pressure tires would dig into the dirt and flip the racer over) so he headed for the main airport at Reno Cannon (now Reno Tahoe) and was disqualified for landing at a field other than the one from which the race was held. However, Greenamyer would be back, and he would go on to become one of the most winning pilots in air race history. His aircraft, F8F-2 BuNo 121646, N1111L, would be modified numerous times over the years by a skilled group of engineers including Bruce Boland and Ray Poe. The plane is seen in its distinctive 1966 blue-and-white color scheme when it won Reno at an average speed of 396.22 miles per hour, starting a run of first-place victories for four years in a row.

On 16 August 1969, Darryl Greenamyer and his crew captured the world absolute propeller-driven speed record—a three-kilometer record that had been held since 1939 by Germany with a specially-built Messerschmitt flown by Fritz Wendel. Recording a blistering 483.041 miles per hour over the Nevada desert, Greenamyer firmly brought the victory to America. Much of the success of race number 1 was due to the aerodynamic work carried out by Greenamyer's crew, especially in the area of the cowling, which was extensively modified to create a better air flow with less drag, while allowing adequate cooling for the R-2800. The plane, now named *Conquest I*, was photographed at Reno during 1970, when Greenamyer placed sixth at an average speed of 297.063 miles per hour. This very slow speed came about because the right main gear would not fully retract. Greenamyer quickly landed, had his single-shot nitrogen bottle refilled (the normal gear mechanism had been removed to save weight), and then took off to rejoin the racers. Once again, the right gear failed to completely retract, but Greenamyer went on to compete even though he knew he would be finishing with a very slow speed.

survivors being relegated to the training mission. Fortunately, the Wildcat was available in squadron strength on the date of the Japanese sneak attack and was able to blunt some of the enemy's seemingly unstoppable force during the early months of fighting. The Wildcat fought through the whole war, its toughness, as well as that of following Grumman fighters, earned the company the nickname of the "Iron Works." The Wildcat was followed by the F6F Hellcat, which scored the highest kill ratio of any fighter in the Pacific, but the later F8F Bearcat was the real feline thoroughbred.

Direct frontal view of *Conquest I* on a snowbound Reno ramp shows some of the details that made N1111L such a record-setter. The clipped wings are immediately evident and are greatly emphasized by the huge propeller blades that came from a Douglas Skyraider and were used to absorb the power generated by the modified R-2800. Note the fit of the spinner and the limited air opening for the air-cooled radial engine—all carefully engineered to cut down on drag while providing adequate cooling.

Conquest I won Reno 1971 at a convincing 413.99 miles per hour, but Greenamyer received several fines for not pulling up after another aircraft declared an emergency and for flying too close to the crowd. This would be the last Reno win for Greenamyer and the 'Cat, which is seen in its new silver paint scheme. Other modifications seen in this view include an increased fillet for the vertical fin and the extended tail cone. The entire airframe had gone through a severe weight-reduction program through the course of its racing history and was at about the absolute limit with the R-2800. However, there were other plans afoot for expanding the Bearcat's performance.

Certainly the most flown of today's Bearcats is Howard Pardue's beautifully maintained XF8F-1 N14HP. In basically stock condition, the Bearcat is still a competitive aircraft because of its high power, small size, and tight turning capabilities (the 'Cat is stressed to plus 7.5 Gs and minus 3.7 Gs). Pardue taxis the XF8F-1 to the active runway at the 1994 Phoenix 500 for one of the heat races. Held at the former Williams Air Force Base, the Phoenix 500 is one of several new air races that are helping the overall popularity of the sport.

LEFT
The last color scheme worn by Greenamyer's Bearcat was a dramatic yellow and orange, with sponsorship provided by American Jet. Photographed during the June 1975 races held at Mojave, the racer is seen undergoing a ground power run. Due to various problems, the best Greenamyer could do was take third in the Gold, with an average speed of 410.68 miles per hour.

With the development of the big twin-engine F7F Tigercat, Leroy Grumman worried that the company was getting away from agile single-engine fighters that could operate off of all classes of Navy carriers. Grumman issued a memo to chief engineer Bill Schwendler during July 1943 to create "a

Reno air racing history changed forever when this aircraft appeared on the ramp during September 1969. Lyle Shelton is seen taxiing out in *Able Cat,* N777L—an aircraft that Shelton had built up from a wreck over a period of years. As can be seen, the plane is relatively stock, but under the cowling was a whole different story, as the R-2800 had been discarded and replaced with a Wright R-3350 mated to a cut-down propeller from a Douglas DC-7 airliner. The R-3350 offered higher horsepower in its stock condition and had a great ability to "grow" with racing modifications. In the 1969 race, Darryl Greenamyer went all-out with a record-setting 412.63 miles per hour, easily beating everyone. Shelton, who was having teething problems with his new mount, placed fifth in the Gold race at 356.37 miles per hour.

small fighter plane, which could (without question) be used on large or small carriers, and with a performance superior to the F6F."

The result was Design 58, whereby Grumman created a "shipborne fighter of minimum weight and maximum perfor-

mance in the low- and medium-altitude range" by mating a small, clean airframe to a powerful and reliable radial engine: the Pratt & Whitney R-2800. The project started with company funding, but the Navy liked what they saw and issued a contract for two proto-

As the years went by, Shelton began refining his new racing aircraft, and when photographed at Reno 1972, the plane had a new purple-and-white paint scheme and clipped wing tips. Also, large wing fillets had been added, and all these modifications helped Shelton attain an average speed of 404.703 miles per hour during the Gold race, but this was not enough to beat Gunther Balz in his highly modified Mustang at 416.160 miles per hour.

PREVIOUS PAGES
High over Mojave, Lyle Shelton slides *Rare Bear* into formation with the Beech Baron camera plane. "I was back to idle power," commented Shelton, "and still sliding past the Baron, which was going full out." As can be seen, at this power setting, the massive propeller appears to be nearly stopped.

types—the first flying on 31 August 1944. Work proceeded at a rapid pace, to go along with the island-hopping war in the Pacific, and the first production variant was the F8F-1. To give an idea of its size, 50 Bearcats could be parked in the same carrier space that was formerly occupied by 36 Hellcats. The first

After undergoing years of modifications, problems, and the occasional victory, Lyle Shelton and his Bearcat, which became known as *Rare Bear*, started, during the late 1980s, to dominate Gold Unlimited racing at Reno. With a characteristic belch of smoke, Shelton brings the R-3350 to life on 11 September 1992 at Mojave, California, prior to a test flight. By this time, the Bearcat had donned a new green-and-white color scheme to reflect the sponsorship of Thomason Aircraft Corporation. Also, the Bearcat sported a new three-blade propeller (the blades being provided from a Lockheed P-3 Orion) that helped transfer the power from the super-hot R-3350 built up by Aircraft Cylinder and Turbine.

Bearcat squadrons were heading for action when the atomic bombings of Hiroshima and Nagasaki ended the World War II. Bearcat production, and production of other warplanes, was slashed—only 293 of the improved F8F-2 variant would be completed.

After the war, jets were the way of the future—even for carrier aircraft. Bearcats put in an appearance with fleet squadrons for a short while before being shuttled off to reserve squadrons, where the "weekend warriors" appreciated the power and agility of their 'Cats. By this time, France was deeply involved in a deadly war in Indochina, and the US government sent off stocks of surplus "obsolete" warplanes to the beleaguered French—including Hellcats, Helldivers, and Bearcats. Thus, the Bearcat never saw action

An aircraft as large and as powerful as *Rare Bear* creates a tremendous amount of wake turbulence, which has to be carefully monitored by pilots flying behind race number 77 (which includes most of the field!). At Reno 1986, hard-charging Skip Holm, piloting *Stiletto,* got behind John Penney in the *Bear,* and the wake turbulence flipped the highly modified Mustang almost on its back. With ultra-quick reactions, Holm jammed in full right rudder, did what the Brits call a "flick roll," and got the Mustang righted a millisecond before impacting the desert floor.

For the 1994 racing season, *Rare Bear* appeared in a brilliant new white and gold race scheme that was elegant as well as eye-catching. The plane is seen during an unseasonable thunderstorm at the first Phoenix 500, held during March. An umbrella shelters the cockpit, while the specially built wing walks (to help protect the wing's slick finish—scratches or imperfections can cost miles per hour) are evident.

with the US Navy, but lots with the French *Armee de l'Air*. When the Korean War came along, the Navy pulled hundreds of Corsairs out of storage and sent the "bent-wing birds" to Korea while the Bearcats stayed home. The Corsair could fill in as a ground-attack air-craft, carrying impressive amounts of under-wing weaponage, where the Bearcat's ground-attack ability was limited. When the French finished with their aircraft, many were transferred to the air forces of the Republic of Vietnam and Thailand.

At the 1995 Phoenix 500, *Rare Bear* was back in style, complete with this souped-up tug. Once again, *Rare Bear* and John Penney would dominate the event. Penney described his qualification run: "I came down the backside and entered the race course like we would on a normal start at about the same indicated air speed. It was very, very tight coming around the backside. This course is an exact race track pattern, a 3,700-foot radius in the turns, with only about a mile and a half on the straight-aways. A small course—a very, very tight course! I was extremely busy trying to maintain visual with all the pylons because they were difficult to see. Without a course where you can maintain an almost constant turn, the airplane, at those speeds, becomes directionally unstable. You've gotta keep fighting the rudder all the time to keep it going straight ahead. After the run, the G meter registered five and a half Gs. One thing that came to mind when I was out there doing about 415 knots indicated on the qualification run which worked out to be about 470 miles per hour, was that I was very busy trying to maintain a good line." Given the difficulties of the race course (which had changed drastically since the crash of the Super Corsair at the 1994 event), Penney was very aware of the other aircraft in the Gold race, so he quickly assumed the lead and finished in first place at 443.372 miles per hour.

John Penney heads out for the 1995 Reno Gold race. *Rare Bear* and Penney had qualified at a stunning new record speed of nearly 490 miles per hour. The race team was hoping for a 500-mile-per-hour record, but there was some trouble with the engine, and it was estimated that power was down by about 500 horsepower. In the Gold race, the problems seemed to be amplified and, try as he might, Penney could not catch Tiger Destefani in *Strega* and finished second at 465.159 miles per hour (which, even though second, was almost 110 miles per hour faster than Shelton's fifth-place finish in the 'Cat at Reno 1969). Note the sheen of oil down the side of the Bearcat's fuselage.

When the reserves began transitioning to jets, surviving F8Fs were sent to Naval Air Station Litchfield Park, Arizona, where they were "pickled" and placed into storage. Unfortunately, there was really no secondary market with third-world air forces, so after several years baking in the desert sun, the majority of the 'Cats had their engines lopped off and saved while the airframes were simply chopped up and melted into aluminum ingots.

A few Bearcats survived to be sold surplus to the civilian sector. However, even though prices were absolutely rock-bottom (in the $2,000 to $3,000 range) there was little interest—more interest was invested in surplus P-51D Mustangs, which could be quickly modified to carry a second seat and were somewhat cheaper to operate.

It was not until 1964, when Bill Stead restarted Unlimited air racing that interest in Bearcats revived. The first event saw two 'Cats dueling for first place—a stock F8F-2 owned by Stead and flown by Mira Slovak, and a much-more-modified aircraft piloted by Darryl Greenamyer. Even though very few Bearcats survived in civilian markings, most would sooner or later make an appearance at the Reno National Air Races. For many years, Greenamyer and his highly modified Bearcat, race number 1, were unbeatable, but this aircraft was eventually retired (and placed in storage in the National Air and Space Museum), and Lyle Shelton began to slowly move forward with his Bearcat, which he had brought back to flying condition from a wreck. Shelton had made one very large change: He had replaced the tried-and-true R-2800 with a Wright R-3350, and as the years went by, Shelton and his talented crew kept refining and modifying the aircraft until, today, *Rare Bear* is the plane to beat at any air race. Currently, Shelton and the *Bear* hold the World Three Kilometer Speed Record, which was set on 22 August 1989 at Las Vegas, Nevada, with an average speed of 528.329 miles per hour.

One of the most attractive of all modified Sea Furys is Howard Pardue's ex-Iraqi Air Force Fury (a de-navalized Sea Fury that was prepared for Iraq and delivered in the early 1950s). During the late 1970s, David Tallichet and Ed Jurist discovered that the Iraqis still had around three dozen Fury airframes and huge quantities of spares, so a deal was struck, and the planes were returned to the United States. A legal dispute prevented the immediate sale of the airframes, but many of these aircraft are now flying; others are under restoration. Pardue obtained his aircraft, which was registered N34SF, in 1984 and had the plane taken to his Breckenridge, Texas, headquarters, where it was handed over to Nelson Ezell's shop for a complete rebuild and conversion to a customized racing/sport machine. Registered NX666HP as race number 66 ("I like sixes," explains the droll Pardue), Nelson replaced all the British systems with more-reliable American units and installed a rebuilt Wright R-3350 with a customized "tuned" exhaust system. The cockpit was also modified to include a second seat under a large bubble canopy. Pardue was very pleased with the result, which was given an unusual Royal Air Force-style camouflage scheme with a massive gold spinner, and has been a regular participant at Reno. At Reno '95, Pardue qualified the Fury at a very respectable seventh with 409.327 miles per hour. At the earlier Phoenix 500 in March, Pardue had installed a radical high-tech propeller for the race. "Slowed the plane down by about 30 miles per hour," stated Pardue. The prop was not in place for Reno. Pardue finished seventh in the '95 Gold Championship Race at 389.131 miles per hour.

CHAPTER THREE

Fury from Hawker

The last of Hawker's long line of piston-engine fighter aircraft would go on to become a potent air racer.

During the dark days of 1940, the Hawker Hurricane, teamed with the Supermarine Spitfire, defeated the threat posed by the Luftwaffe as Hitler planned his invasion of Britain. The Hurricane, Britain's first production monoplane fighter with retractable landing gear and an enclosed cockpit, was in itself a logical progression of Hawker's elegant Fury biplane.

The Hurricane was followed by the massive Typhoon and Tempest fighters—heavy hitters that were also employed by the Royal Air Force in the ground-attack role. The Hawker Fury evolved from a proposal titled "Tempest Light Fighter (Centaurus)." Using the Bristol Centaurus sleeve-valve 18-cylinder powerplant, a sleek monoplane standing on a wide-track landing gear was envisioned. Work began in late 1942, but Hawker and the Air Ministry had differing ideas over the project. However, the differences were eventually worked out and the Royal Air Force and Royal Navy showed interest in the result.

Hawker's chief designer was Sydney Camm (who would be knighted for his many aeronautical accomplishments in 1953), and he planned that the first few prototypes of the new design would be used to test different powerplants. Named the Fury, the first aircraft flew on 1 September 1944 with Philip Lucas in the cockpit. After test flights with different engines, it was decided to concentrate development on the Centaurus engine.

However, victory in Europe was near at hand, and all 200 Royal Air Force Furys were canceled outright. In the meantime, the Royal Navy's version, the Sea Fury, pro-

The ultimate Hawker Sea Fury racer is, without doubt, the Sanders *Dreadnought*, brainchild of Frank Sanders and his family, long time owners of Sea Furys. The concept for *Dreadnought* came about when Sanders began contemplating mating the big and rugged Sea Fury airframe with America's biggest production piston-engine powerplant: the Pratt & Whitney R-4360 Wasp Major. In 1939, Pratt & Whitney, like most American aviation concerns, was a struggling business, but desperate British and French orders quickly added needed cash. Pratt & Whitney began developing a wide variety of powerplants, hoping to branch into liquid-cooled engines. However, such a development project would be a huge undertaking, and Pratt & Whitney was enjoying some major successes with its new R-2800 so the company and the US Army Air Corps jointly agreed to let Pratt & Whitney stick to air-cooled radials, and the groundwork for the massive R-4360 was begun. By June 1942, the new engine had passed its first test and was developing a stunning 3,000 horsepower, while its growth potential was very high. With four rows of cylinders (comprising 28 cylinders, a one-piece crankshaft, and split master rods), cooling was a major problem, so Pratt & Whitney "swirled" the cylinders in a pattern that gave the engine the nickname "corncob." By the end of World War II, Pratt & Whitney had built the amazing total of 363,619 aircraft engines developing 603,814,723 horsepower! Rick Brickert is seen displaying *Dreadnought*'s classic lines during May 1986.

ceeded, since it could be used in the upcoming final battle with Japan. The first Sea Fury flew on 21 February 1945. Big and powerful, the Sea Fury held its own in the dawn of the new jet age, and Hawker had orders for 565 aircraft by 1950, with many aircraft being finished as fighter-bombers designated FB Mk. 11. Too late for service in World War II, the Sea Fury went into action in Korea, flying thousands of missions

Frank Sanders had obtained the fairly complete airframe of Burmese Air Force T. Mk. 20 VZ368 (serialed UB-451 in Burmese service) and had the aircraft stored in its wooden shipping crate at the family's Chino, California, hangar during 1979. The two-seater was an ideal candidate for Sanders' project, so the Centaurus engine was removed, the airframe thoroughly cleaned and stripped, and a search begun for missing components while Sanders began tackling the engineering needed for the conversion. There was no doubt that the big Sea Fury could handle the R-4360, but problems such as a new cowling, motor mount, propeller, and new internal systems all had to be solved. By the end of its development life, the R-4360 was developing well over 4,000 horsepower, and in the early 1980s complete engines were available, along with a strong parts supply. With the help of sons Dennis and Brian and wife Ruth, work on the new racing aircraft began to proceed rapidly. Sanders also subcontracted some of the work to the vast aviation talent pool at Chino.

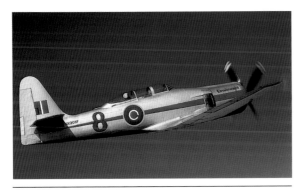

Sanders put lots of detail work into his new racer, some of which is not readily visible at first glance. For example, the rather clunky two-seat canopy arrangement was subtly refined to produce a unit that created much less drag than the normal canopies. As usual, the British air-brake system was dispensed with in favor of much-more-efficient American equipment, including brakes from an F-102. The completed aircraft made its first flight from Chino on 6 August 1983, and few problems were encountered. However, it soon became apparent that a larger vertical stabilizer and rudder were needed to handle the increased power and larger propeller, so the vertical surfaces were suitably enlarged. The two-seat, dual-control configuration was retained (unique for an all-out Unlimited, but Sanders wanted the aircraft to be useful as a possible high-speed test bed). *Dreadnought* created a sensation when it arrived on the ramp at Reno 1983. Finished in a sparkling Royal Air Force scheme of silver and red, *Dreadnought* was one of 32 Unlimited aircraft set to qualify that year. In the cockpit was General Dynamics executive Neil Anderson, an ex-Marine Corps fighter pilot and test pilot for the F-16. However, Anderson was regarded as a rookie because he had never raced in an Unlimited event. Anderson took *Dreadnought* out on the 9.187-mile course and hit 446.39 miles per hour, making him the fastest qualifier. Anderson did not hold back in Sunday's Gold race and went on to win at 425.24 miles per hour. Over the years, *Dreadnought* has been a regular Unlimited participant and has enjoyed its share of success, but the big Sea Fury has been partially eclipsed by *Rare Bear* and the new generation of highly modified Mustangs. At Reno 1995, Dennis Sanders qualified the racer at 434.667 miles per hour, which put the plane in fifth place (giving some idea how Unlimited speeds had increased since *Dreadnought*'s first Reno outing). Immediately after winning the Gold heat race on 14 September (at 426.122 miles per hour), Sanders declared a Mayday and safely put the racer down on the runway—after years of faithful performance, the big R-4360 had finally come apart, and *Dreadnought* was on the ground for the rest of Reno 1995. Here, Ruth Sanders is seen flying *Dreadnought* from the rear cockpit during May 1987.

against the enemy and even successfully engaging and destroying the enemy's new MiG-15 jet fighter.

The Sea Fury was also an export success, with examples going to Canada, Australia, Egypt, Iraq, The Netherlands, Pakistan, and Burma. Many Sea Furys soldiered on into the late 1950s and early 1960s. When the warbird movement began to take hold in the United States during the mid-1960s, a Sea Fury could be purchased for a few thousand dollars, but it was not considered worth the cost to bring the plane back into the country!

After blowing the R-4360 in a practice run at Reno 1983, Lloyd Hamilton and his crew were back in 1984 with a much better prepared race number 15. The aircraft was now finished in a very attractive red-and-gold color scheme with the new name *Furias*. However, the racing gods were not looking kindly on the R-4360 Sea Furys. Neil Anderson in *Dreadnought* was forced out with engine problems after a 429.9mph qualifying run, and Hamilton and *Furias* experienced their own unique set of problems. Noticing engine vibrations, Hamilton pulled up high over the Reno runways but the engine violently "sneezed," blowing virtually all the cowling off the R-4360! Hamilton executed an extremely skillful emergency landing, and the stricken racer (note the oil pouring out of the engine) is seen being towed back to the pits. Race number 15 was most definitely out of the running.

Two Sea Furys were imported during the mid-1960s, and both hit the race circuit, where they proved that they were fast machines. Accordingly, as the years went by and prices began to escalate, more Sea Furys were imported. Certainly Sanders Aircraft must be credited with putting the Sea Fury on the map when it came to air racing. Their masterful mating of a Pratt & Whitney R-4360 with a two-seat Sea Fury created *Dreadnought*—one of the most powerful of all air racers.

The past few years of air racing have seen *Dreadnought* eclipsed by *Rare Bear* and *Strega*, but the racing Sea Furys are still machines that command respect by all who race against them.

Race number 15 was back at Reno 1985 with a rebuilt engine and several other improvements. The Gold race that year was most interesting because it featured three R-4360-powered racers: *Dreadnought* with Neil Anderson, the Super Corsair with Steve Hinton, and Hamilton with *Furias*. In a hard-fought battle, Anderson appeared to be the winner, but he had cut a pylon, so Hinton was declared winner of the 9.222-mile, eight-lap race at 438.186 miles per hour. Only four racers finished the race, with *Furias* coming in fourth at 411.952 miles per hour. As with *Dreadnought*, *Furias* needed more vertical tail area, so Lloyd Hamilton's crew added a swept-back fin cap. At the 1986 Reno event, Hamilton and *Furias* placed second in the Gold race at 429.374 miles per hour—the aircraft's best showing. At Reno 1987, Hamilton and *Furias* placed fifth at 403.632 miles per hour. *Furias* was soon retired and has been in storage ever since.

Another early Sea Fury owner was Mike Carroll, who obtained FB Mk. 11 WG567, CF-VAN, from Canada in 1965. The plane had operated with the Royal Canadian Navy before being surplused. Registered N878M by Carroll, the aircraft was put through Vern Barker's Pylon Air facility at Long Beach, California, and emerged as one of the first "all-out" Unlimited air racers. The craft had all military equipment removed, airframe lightened, outer wing panels clipped (eliminating 6-1/2 feet total), a small bubble canopy installed, and a wild paint scheme that made the Sea Fury look every inch a racer. The new racer made its first appearance at Reno 1966, having been "borrowed" by Lyle Shelton, who qualified at 364.08 miles per hour but cut a pylon, which dropped him into the Silver race. The plane still retained its original air braking system, and this caused Shelton lots of problems during ground operations. In the Silver, Shelton was passed by a Bearcat, and then a Mustang, but Shelton poured on the power to finish second at 353.89 miles per hour. In 1967, Reno had a transcontinental race from Rockford, Illinois, to Reno and this was won handily by Mike Carroll in N878M, averaging an excellent 418.223 miles per hour over the 1,609.74 miles. Carroll was also having Pylon Air rebuild the rare Bell P-39 Airacobra that had been raced at Cleveland as *Cobra II*. The Airacobra had been exotically modified, and Carroll had lots of hope for the new racer, but tragically, the plane developed mechanical problems on its first flight one month prior to Reno 1968. Carroll bailed out of the stricken racer but hit the tail and was killed. The Airacobra crashed into the Navy's nuclear-weapons storage facility at Seal Beach and was totally destroyed.

Carroll's estate sold his Sea Fury to Dr. Sherman Cooper of Merced, California, who changed the name to *Miss Merced*. Cooper took the Sea Fury to Reno 1970, where he won the Silver race at 361.8 miles per hour and then entered the craft in the California 1000—a strange 1970 event at Mojave, California, that saw the racers go 1,000 miles around a pylon course. Needless to say, some of the 34 aircraft entered (20 eventually started the race) had to land, refuel, then take off again, which added to the confusion. *Miss Merced*, with its large fuel capacity, was able to take first place—five laps ahead of the second place rival—with a top speed of 344.41 miles per hour. In 1971, the event was repeated at San Diego's Brown Field (which required one mandatory fuel stop to give the shorter-range racers more of a chance). Even so, Cooper once again dominated, at 330 miles per hour. The 1971 season was very busy with an air race at Cape May, New Jersey, followed by Reno, where Cooper finished third at 412.583 miles per hour in a Gold race that saw the top four aircraft all finishing within four seconds of each other. The 1971 race season closed out at Mojave with a new 1,000-kilometer race (621 miles). Seventeen aircraft were entered, and Cooper was once again favored to win, but the Centaurus engine gave up the ghost, so Cooper put the plane down in a very hard crash landing that inflicted heavy damage to the racer. Cooper was later killed in the crash of a Pitts Special biplane, and the wreck was purchased by Frank Sanders, then sold to James Mott, who eventually rebuilt the plane as race number 42, *Super Chief*, and as such, it enjoyed an undistinguished attempt at Unlimited racing before being put up for sale.

At Reno 1995, the Sanders *Parts Fury* was flown by Brian Sanders to qualify at 380.951 miles per hour. This aircraft was built up by Brian and Dennis as a spare-time project, using parts and bits and pieces they had accumulated over the years. Since the aircraft was a ground-up rebuild, the brothers took their time to Americanize all systems and to mount a Wright R-3350 up front in place of the Bristol. The R-3350 seems to be the engine of choice for American Sea Fury owners, who want a bit more power and who do not want to cater to the somewhat eccentric Bristol. During one of the Unlimited heats at Reno 1995, the *Parts Fury* was flown by Lloyd Hamilton with the blessing of the Sanders brothers so that Hamilton's string of participation at Reno would not be broken. Brian Sanders flew the *Parts Fury* in the Unlimited Championship Race at Reno '95, but the aircraft was hard-pressed to keep up with the fully modified Unlimiteds such as *Dago Red*, *Strega*, and *Rare Bear*, so Sanders had to be content with a next-to-last finish, at 366.055 miles per hour. As can be seen, the *Parts Fury* is fitted in this photograph with Sanders Smokewinders, which are particularly useful if and when the Sea Fury is used as a pace plane for starting Unlimited races.

RIGHT
Detailed view of the Wright R-3350 in Pardue's Fury. Although the Wrights have replaced the Bristol Centaurus radials in most American-operated Sea Furys, the Bristol is a famous engine in its own right. The largest British radial to enter production in World War II, the 18-cylinder two-row radial dispenses with the more common poppet valves in favor of sleeves. The engine has a displacement of 3,270 cubic inches and has a standard military rating of 2,470 horsepower at 2700 rpm for takeoff. Design for the Wright R-3350 began as long ago as 1936, and a prototype engine was run by 1937. Numerous problems, including catastrophic backfires, delayed development, but the engine was chosen for the new Boeing B-29 Superfortress, so development of the engine was given a top priority. However, fuel injection, which would have solved many of the problems, had to wait until the end of the war. Variants of the R-3350 were used on Constellations, Skyraiders, DC-7s, and other aircraft and "growth" variants of the radial increased power to an amazing 3,700 horsepower!

A wildly painted (actually, it wasn't paint but a temporary colored wax) Iraqi Fury is seen taxiing out for the second Phoenix 500 race on 23 March 1995. Held at the former Williams Air Force Base, located near Phoenix, Arizona, the two Phoenix 500 events held up to the time of this book attracted a good selection of racers and spectators. Fury FB Mk. 10 NX24SF is fitted with a Wright R-3350 and is owned by Chuck Leshe of Chandler, Arizona. At the Phoenix race, the Fury was flown by Nelson Ezell.

One of the most radical racers to appear on the 1987 Reno ramp was NX85SF, race number 88, a highly modified T. Mk. 20S (ex-German registration D-COTE). This aircraft had been obtained in 1984 and was rebuilt as *Blind Man's Bluff* by Eric Lorentzen (who owned a window-blind company, hence the name). Fitted with an R-3350 designed to run on alcohol, with a cowl from a Douglas A-26, the plane had a set-back cockpit, a vertical tail increased by 14 inches, and cut-down outer wing panels that reduced with span to 34.5 feet. It was originally planned to have an active US Air Force female pilot race the plane, but the US Air Force would not go along with the idea. Instead, air-show pilot Joann Osterud was the replacement, but her dismal performance in pilot qualifications called for yet another replacement pilot. In the meantime, all the alcohol-fuel modifications were doing was destroying perfectly good R-3350s. The replacement pilot was none other than Skip Holm who did everything in his power to make a very sick airplane perform (a conventional R-3350 was installed in place of the modified engine) and qualified the craft at 394 miles per hour. The dismal, not to say costly, performance of this aircraft quickly resulted in the owner selling the plane, and it went through several owners and a belly landing before being purchased by Tom Dwelle, an ex-Skyraider pilot, who rebuilt the craft at his Auburn, California, facility. Back on the ramp at Reno 1993 and renamed *Critical Mass*, the highly modified racer was enjoying better success. However, in 1995 the racer was heavily damaged when a high-pressure bottle in the fuselage burst, Dwelle losing several fingers in the process. Fortunately, both are on the mend, and Dwelle vows to have the craft back on the air-race circuit.

By 1993, Kevin Eldridge had taken over piloting the Super Corsair (which, like most of the big Unlimiteds, had received various small modifications over the years in order to improve its performance), and the aircraft is seen on the ramp at Reno 1993. This view emphasizes the massive cowling and R-4360, pretty much negating the pilot's forward view while on the ground. Also, the small fillet on the vertical tail and fillets on the wing roots are readily visible.

CHAPTER FOUR

Super Corsair

This highly modified Corsair recalled the immediate postwar years of Unlimited racing, when Goodyear F2G Super Corsairs dominated the Cleveland pylons.

On 25 October 1944, during the invasion of the Philippines, nine Japanese Zero fighters took off from Mabalcat airfield and headed over the Pacific. Their target was the American fleet and the nine enemy pilots were not going back to their home field after the raid. Five of the Zeros were going to be part of the newly created *Shimpu Tokubetsu Kogekita* (Divine Wind), a suicide corps of volunteer pilots whose mission would be to dive into the ships of the American fleet—especially the aircraft carriers. The other four aircraft would serve as escorts. The nine young pilots wore a traditional *hachimaki* scarf wrapped around their heads. Samurai warriors once wore these headbands to keep their long hair out of their faces during combat. The pilots had taken last rites before the mission and had been told personally by Admiral Takijiro Onishi, who had come up with the human-bomb concept, that, "You are already gods without earthly desires!"

The kamikazes found the American fleet, and as Corsair fighters launched off the decks of carriers to intercept the low-flying enemy, Lieutenant Seki dove his Zero into the flight deck of the escort carrier USS *St. Lo*. The explosion shook the ship, setting off further explosions and attracting the attention of the other kamikazes, two of which dove

The 1980s were a decade of positive advancement for Unlimited air racing. Not only did speeds take a major jump forward during this time but a number of new and innovative racing aircraft were constructed, flown, and raced. During the 1950s, aviation enthusiast Ed Maloney was gathering aircraft and artifacts that no one wanted—planes that were being threatened with the scrap heap. These aircraft were to become the basis for The Air Museum, the first aviation museum in the western United States. Among the artifacts gathered by Maloney was the fuselage of a Vought F4U-1D Corsair, acquired from a movie studio. The Air Museum already had a flyable Corsair, and in the early 1980s Steve Hinton and Jim Maloney surveyed the fuselage and decided it would make an excellent basis for a new Unlimited racer. Hinton, Jim Maloney, and many of the talented individuals call Chino home went to work on the project. Two wings were obtained, one coming from Central America in poor shape but it was redone and metalized (Corsairs had fabric covering over the majority of the wing surface) by Dennis Sanders. John Sandberg supplied the rebuilt Pratt & Whitney R-4360, and a new cowling was fabricated. Registered NX31518, the "new" Super Corsair is pictured airborne with Steve Hinton at the controls near Chino in September 1982, prior to its first appearance at Reno.

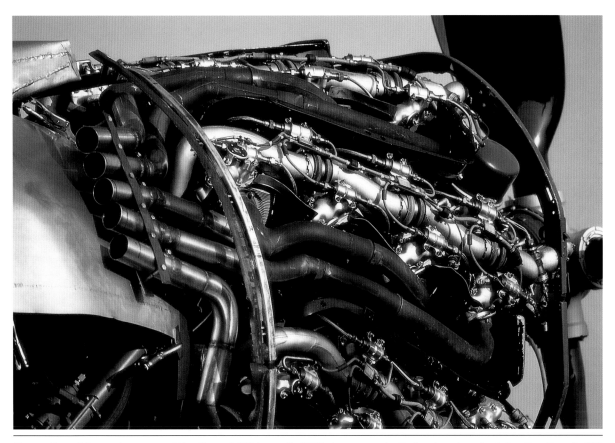

Super Corsair's motive power: The Pratt & Whitney R-4360 that was rebuilt for the plane by John Sandberg's JRS shop is seen after first engine runs during August 1982.

into the ship while three other escort carriers were also attacked. The *St. Lo* sank, and the Americans were stunned. Something would have to be done to combat this new weapon.

What was needed was a high-speed low-altitude interceptor that could get to the enemy aircraft before they reached the perimeter of the fleet's defensive anti-aircraft fire. The Americans were soon losing more ships than they had lost since the Pearl Har-

bor attack as fanatical Japanese made death plunges into the warships.

American military planners saw that the F4U-4 was not the ideal aircraft for interception of these surprise attacks. The Corsairs stopped many of the enemy, but a lighter and more responsive aircraft was needed that could quickly be scrambled and head at high speed toward the oncoming attackers and destroy them before they

Right down to the line, Steve Hinton, Jim Maloney, and their crew install the right wing on the Super Corsair in late August 1982 before the aircraft's first flight. The crew was working nonstop to get the plane to Reno. This photograph of the unpainted airframe shows some details to advantage including the clipped wings, metalized wing surfaces, new cowl and exhaust, Skyraider propeller, and modified windshield and canopy. The Super Corsair and P-51D *Dago Red* were both new to Reno 1982, and both planes were big hits—the Super Corsair representing pure, raw horsepower while *Dago* was an extension of the Mustang's airframe sleekness. Painted in an attractive blue-and-silver scheme, the Super Corsair, carrying race number 1, was qualified by Steve Hinton at 413.21 miles per hour and would be raced alternately by Hinton and Jim Maloney. Sponsorship had been obtained from Budweiser for the Gold Championship, and Hinton was at the controls and finished the eight-lap race in fourth place at 362.50 miles per hour. The Super Corsair would become a dependable regular at Reno and other races, but its moment of true glory came at Reno 1985 when Hinton won the Gold Championship at 438.186 miles per hour.

Steve Hinton breaks away from the camera plane, illustrating the Super Corsair's clipped wings, huge engine and cowling, and other details such as the recontoured air inlets for the oil coolers. At Reno 1987, John Maloney was at the controls of race number 1, coming in fourth in the Gold Championship at 416.905 miles per hour. Maloney went on to become the regular pilot of the Super Corsair and was a consistent competitor in the Championship race, always placing in the money, but the Super Corsair had been eclipsed by *Rare Bear*, *Strega*, and *Tsunami*.

reached the ships. Goodyear, who built Corsairs under license, teamed with Vought and Pratt & Whitney to mate an R-4360 engine to a lightened Corsair airframe. Orders for 418 F2G-1s were placed with Goodyear, but problems were soon encountered, as the prototypes could not reach their projected 450 mile per hour top speeds and were unstable on the lateral axis. Also, Pratt & Whitney was having problems producing the engine. Contracts were rapidly let, but only five F2G-1s (fixed wings) and five F2G-2s (folding wings) were built.

In 1994, the first Phoenix 500 Air Race was held at the former Williams Air Force Base outside Phoenix. The event attracted a goodly number of Unlimiteds, including the Super Corsair. Kevin Eldridge qualified the plane, which was having some engine problems, in fourth place at 428.104 miles per hour. It was decided to hold two Unlimited heats on Saturday, and the second race saw the dramatic demise of the Super Corsair. Under a heavy overcast, the race started out in normal fashion with Howard Pardue taking the lead in his Fury with Eldridge tight on his tail. On the fourth lap, a long plume of white smoke came out of the Super Corsair's engine. More smoke came forth and Eldridge pulled up and out, declaring a Mayday. As he went for altitude, a huge gush of flame poured from under the aircraft and then went out. However, another burst of flame followed before it was extinguished. Robbie Patterson and Bob Hoover were flying in the TF-51D safety aircraft, and they pulled alongside the stricken Super Corsair. By this time, flame was once again pouring from the R-4360. "From my position in formation, I could feel the intense heat," commented Patterson. Eldridge was apparently getting out of his seat harness and the nose of the Super Corsair momentarily dropped. The nose came up, but the plane began rolling to the right, and the fire in the engine area burned unchecked. The spectators clearly saw Eldridge exit the blazing Super Corsair and were relieved moments later when the parachute opened.

What they did not know was that Eldridge had struck the tail, breaking an arm, leg, and two discs in his neck. The Super Corsair dove into the ground and exploded, while Eldridge drifted down to safely land in a field. Rescue workers were soon on the scene and Eldridge was rushed to a hospital. He needed several months of recuperation, but he recovered from his injuries and was soon again back flying. Of the Super Corsair, there was little left. Steve Hinton dragged some of the remains back to Chino where, with Eldridge in attendance, the bits and pieces were given a ceremonial burial at the birthplace of one of the most interesting of all Unlimiteds. The era of the Super Corsair was over.

After the war, several of these fighters survived the mass scrapings and were purchased surplus for use in the post-war Cleveland Thompson Trophy Races. Cook Cleland entered several of these aircraft and won the 1947 Thompson in F2G N5577N, race number 74, at 396.131 miles per hour, while Dick Becker came in second in F2G N5590N, race number 94, at 390.133 miles per hour. In the 1948 Thompson, race numbers 74 and 94 both pulled out with mechanical problems. One of the F2Gs was lost in a fatal accident, but by the 1949 race, the last Unlimited air race until the start of the Reno races, the Super Corsairs were in fine form. Cleland had cut down his Super Corsair's wingspan to a mere 33.2 feet and added a hydrogen-peroxide injection system to the engine, which was expected to help the engine to pull 4,000 horsepower out of the R-4360 when running at 2800 rpm. The modifications proved useful, and Cleland won the event in race number 94 at 397.071 miles per hour, while Ron Puckett took second at 393.527 miles per hour in F2G N91092, race number 18, and Ben McKillen got third in F2G N5588N, race number 57, at 387.589 miles per hour. After the 1949 Cleveland Air Races, the Super Corsairs were basically shoved into the weeds and left to rot. It would not be until the early 1980s that another Super Corsair would return to Unlimited air racing.

Rookie Bob "Buckwheat" Hannah of Caldwell, Idaho, qualified the Museum of Flying's Republic P-47D Thunderbolt, race number 47, at 324.641 miles per hour at the 1995 Phoenix 500 and went on to finish fourth in the Silver stock race at 258.482 miles per hour and went into the Gold stock race the same day, 26 March, where he finished fifth at 263.205 miles per hour. The big Thunderbolt, being flown by Tiger Destefani in this photograph, is accompanied by Robert Converse's P-51D race number 71, *Huntress III*.

CHAPTER FIVE

They Also Raced

Over the years, Unlimited air racing has seen a wide variety of contestants—ranging from exotic warbirds, to homebuilts with big engines, to purpose-built pylon racers.

Since the rebirth of Unlimited air racing at Reno in 1964, a wide variety of aircraft have made their appearances around the racing pylons. In the early years, the value of some of the aircraft that would be known as warbirds was limited, so rare planes such as P-38 Lightnings, Bell P-39 Airacobras and P-63 Kingcobras, and Republic P-47 Thunderbolts made occasional appearances. However, as the monetary value of some of these rare planes began to rapidly escalate, owners were less willing to risk putting the craft around the pylons because air racing always carries an implied threat of damage or destruction. In the long run, however, Unlimited air racing has had a safer record than just the nor-

mal operations of warbird-type aircraft. The reason for this is twofold: Unlimited pilots are usually highly skilled individuals, and their aircraft are also usually prepared to the highest, most exacting standards.

Over the years, Reno, along with other Unlimited racing venues, has hosted a variety of unusual aircraft including some homebuilts, but these aircraft have never even placed and apparently have been entered more for the owner's ego than for any true attempt at pylon-racing success. Kitplanes such the Lancairs and Glasairs, while extremely good and fast general-aviation aircraft, simply do not have what it takes to compete with the World War II-era racing

During World War II, the majority of Bell P-63 Kingcobra production was sent to Russia as part of the Lend-Lease program because the US government did not want to supply the Russians with better fighters, such as the P-51 Mustang. After the war, P-63s that had been retained by the USAAF as advanced fighter trainers were surplused off—the average price being $500. P-63C USAAF s/n 44-4393 was sold as NX62822 and participated in the post-war Thompson Trophy event as race number 17. After a period of storage, the aircraft was obtained by John Sandberg in 1969 and highly modified as race number 28, with the name *Tipsy Miss*. The airframe was constantly being modified by Sandberg, and a variety of Allison V-1710 V-12s was also tried since Sandberg also owned his own engine shop. The attractive aircraft was never really a contender, so in 1975 it was sold to Mike Smith, who is seen piloting the aircraft during October 1977. Race modifications such as the clipped wing (chopped from 39.2 feet to 31 feet and which also had all panel lines filled and sanded smooth), clipped horizontal, wing fillets, and modified exhaust system are evident.

machinery. Also, in recent years, high-performance trainer aircraft such as the North American T-28 Trojan have been entered. While some of these have actually qualified, once again, they simply do not have what it takes. In this chapter we will look at some of the exotics, but because of space, will exclude the larger multi-engine aircraft—Douglas A-26 Invader, Douglas DC-7, and Lockheed Constellation (the two four-engine aircraft raced in the 1,000-mile/kilometer events)—and the homebuilts and kitplanes.

During the late 1970s, three of air racing's most creative individuals—Bruce Boland, Ray Poe, and John Sandberg—combined forces to create *Tsunami*, an aircraft that

The most modified Kingcobra to ever race was Larry Havens's N9009 race number 90, which is seen on the Reno ramp during September 1971. This aircraft had been extensively modified by Pylon Air with drastically clipped wings, a hot Allison, and miniature canopy. Starting out life as P-63C USAAF s/n 44-4181, the Kingcobra was sold surplus as NX73744 and competed at Cleveland as race number 53. In 1969, the Kingcobra was one of several ex-Cleveland P-63s obtained by Darryl Greenamyer, but the project was sold to Larry Havens, who used parts from all the airframes to create the new racer. Although the plane showed potential, finishing fourth in the Silver race, Havens had an unfortunate incident while preparing for the 1972 Reno event (which was scheduled to have three Bell racers, the most since Cleveland). While out on a test flight over the Pacific Ocean, Havens felt a bang from the rear of the aircraft. Apparently, the engine had backfired, collapsing the induction system. This appeared to have damaged the controls, so Havens bailed out at 3,500 feet and was picked up by a boat. The Kingcobra plunged into the ocean and sank in 200 feet of water.

As mentioned, Reno 1972 was scheduled to host three Bell racers: Kingcobras race number 28 and race number 90 and Bell P-39 Airacobra N40A, race number 21, the first time a P-39 had raced since Cleveland. This particular aircraft was built as P-39Q USAAF s/n 44-3908 and, sometime during its military life, had been converted to a dual-control TP-39Q. The plane was sold surplus after the war as NX4829N and participated as race number 15 at Cleveland. Purchased by E. D. Weiner in 1957 as N40A, the aircraft was stored at Orange County Airport, California, from 1959 to 1971, when it was discovered and purchased by Mira Slovak, winner of the first Reno Unlimited event held in 1964. Slovak wanted to modify the aircraft for racing, and he obtained the sponsorship of Mennen Inc. Rebuilt at Van Nuys, California, the plane emerged in gleaming white and green with the name *Mr. Mennen* and the race number 21 on its tail. As can be seen, the aircraft did not have its airframe drastically altered, but it did have a very hot Allison installed, and great things were expected of the new racer. Unfortunately, Mira arrived after the deadline. Reno officials decided to play hardball and would not allow the racer to participate, thus losing an interesting aircraft and a very major sponsor—something that Unlimited air racing could not afford to lose. Disgusted with Reno, Slovak sold the racer and it first went to the Confederate Air Force and then to the Kalamazoo Aviation History Museum, where it is now on display.

many thought would be the future of air racing. Sandberg had entered a bright red-orange Bell P-63 Kingcobra in numerous races but, although the aircraft was constantly being modified, it simply was not competitive and seemed to exist to "eat" Allison V-12s—which it did in prodigious quantities. Flown by a variety of skilled pilots, *Tsunami* required years to begin to show its

One of the most popular Unlimited aircraft is also one of the most historic. Lefty Gardner is seen flying his Lockheed P-38 Lightning N25Y—an aircraft that has come to be identified with Reno, both as a racer and as an airshow performer because Gardner puts the Lightning through some of the most graceful of aerobatics to thrill spectators. N25Y was built as P-38L USAAF s/n 44-53254 and surplused to J. D. Reed of Houston, Texas, who converted the aircraft to Cleveland Bendix race number 14 with the name *Sky Ranger*. The plane went through several modifications and paint schemes and was one of the most competitive and attractive of the racing Lightnings. After Cleveland, the racer went through several owners, on a gradual downhill trend, but it was purchased by Lefty Gardner in 1964 and acquired the red-white-and-blue paint scheme of the Confederate Air Force, of which Gardner was a founding member. Over the years, the P-38 has carried the name *White Lightnin* and has raced as number 25 and number 13. Gardner announced a retirement in 1994 but fortunately, this proved premature, and Gardner, who probably has more flight time in P-38s than any other individual, and his Lightning continue to grace the sky.

Reno 1984 saw the usual pack of hot-rod Unlimiteds but one of the most unusual aircraft to round the pylons was Wiley Sanders's North American B-25 Mitchell. Wildly outclassed, the bomber did manage to qualify and was popular with the fans, who enjoyed the spectacle and sound of the Mitchell trundling around the pylons.

true potential. Some have said that the plane was always being over-engineered, thus hurting its sole purpose of being an out-and-out pylon racer. Just before the plane claimed the life of Sandberg in a nonracing-related crash, *Tsunami* was finally coming into its own.

With the collapse of the former Soviet Union, a variety of former communist aircraft have become available on the American market, and one of the most popular for air racing has been the two-seat Yakovlev Yak-11 advanced trainer. Numerous attempts, some disastrous, have been undertaken with the Yak-11 to turn it into an Unlimited pylon racer. One of the most successful, Bob

Yancey's (powered by a Pratt & Whitney R-2800), was purchased in November 1995 to become part of Alan Preston's new three-Yak racing team. Preston, responsible for the elegant *Stiletto* and, more recently, the new production Yak-3 fighters, plans to field modified Yaks in the Bronze, Silver, and Gold categories.

Unlimited pylon racing has taken many different forms to accomplish the same goal: ultimate speed. One of the most unusual was the Pond Racer, built for aircraft collector, former US Navy pilot, and industrialist Bob Pond. Designed at Mojave, Cali-

John Paul of Boise, Idaho, has been a long-time attendee of the Reno Air Races, often bringing one of his rare Curtiss P-40s. The P-40, certainly a classic fighter, is by no means competitive, but the spectators love seeing the Allison-powered beauty turn the pylons. For Reno 1995, Paul treated the crowd by bring both of his P-40s, and during the Sunday Bronze race both P-40s flew, one being piloted by Tom Camp, the other by Lefty Gardner. Camp dropped out with fouled plugs, but Gardner finished in fourth place.

LEFT

One of the rarest aircraft to be seen on the racing circuit is the Supermarine Spitfire. One of World War II's classic fighting aircraft, the Spitfire is, today, a rare commodity and probably too valuable to race—not to mention the fact that the plane really does not have what it takes for the Silver or Gold events. At the 1995 Phoenix 500, a stock racing category was established so that fans would see how fighters of various types would compete without resorting to race power settings. Santa Monica's Museum of Flying entered their two Spitfires, a Mk. IX and a Mk. XIV—both of which had appropriate racing numbers. In the background is the Museum's P-47D Thunderbolt.

BELOW

For many air-race enthusiasts, the aircraft that seemed capable of replacing the warbirds in the Unlimited Racing category was the elegant JRS *Tsunami*. The design, which some referred to as a modernized Mustang, was the brainchild of Lockheed Skunk Works engineer Bruce Boland. Boland got together with John Sandberg, and a partnership was formed that would see the birth of one of the most exciting air racers in decades. In this May 1987 photograph, Steve Hinton is piloting *Tsunami* over a Chino cloud bank.

Tsunami being pushed out of the Fighter Rebuilders hangar at Chino, California, for one of its early test flights, in September 1986. Boland assembled a team including Ray Poe, Pete Law, and many other talented individuals who would eventually bring the new airplane to life. The project began on 1 November 1979. Proceeding at a craftsman-like pace, the partially completed aircraft was transferred to Chino for installation of systems, completion of airframe work, and installation of the specially modified JRS Merlin. Taxi tests were started on 13 August 1986, and the first flight, with Steve Hinton at the controls, happened on 17 August. With 40 hours of test flying completed, the racer went to Reno, where Hinton qualified the plane at 435 miles per hour. However, a minor engine problem caused Hinton to pull up and out of the Gold Championship Race. Each year would see *Tsunami* undergo a series of modifications as John Sandberg strove for absolute aeronautical perfection. With a wingspan of 27.6 feet, a wing area of 146 square feet, and a length of 28.6 feet, *Tsunami* was just about the smallest package that could handle a full-race Merlin. For Reno 1987, Hinton qualified the silver-and-blue racer at 464.65 miles per hour. However, he was edged out by Tiger Destefani at nearly 467 miles per hour. During the Gold race, the Merlin suffered a mechanical problem. On landing one of the gear legs failed, and *Tsunami* slewed around in a damaging ground loop. At Reno 1988, *Tsunami* and Hinton finished the Gold Championship Race in third place at 429.947 miles per hour.

fornia, by Burt Rutan, the Pond Racer was unusual in every aspect—from its basic configuration to its powerplants, two highly modified automotive engines. Unleashed creativity does not always bring success, and the Pond Racer seemed unable to compete no matter how much money was fed into the project. The best the aircraft ever did was to come in second to a stock Mustang in a Reno Bronze event. The fact that the aircraft eventually claimed the life of the popular and talented Rick Brickert is one that still rankles the majority of professional Unlimited pilots.

As of this writing (January 1996), new projects are underway to create the ultimate pylon racer. Matt Jackson and

Some critics have stated that *Tsunami* was being over-engineered by the various modifications undertaken each year. However, one would be hard-pressed to have a more dedicated crew working on the aircraft. At Reno 1989, *Tsunami* was recovering from extensive damage incurred in an attempt on the absolute world speed record for prop-driven aircraft. Hinton managed to qualify at 462 miles per hour, but the racing Merlin came apart and had to be replaced with the engine that had survived the crash-landing during the speed run. Hinton dropped out on the seventh lap of the Gold Championship and posted a low 385.754 miles per hour.

Tsunami and Hinton scored their first victory in the Gold at the one-off 1990 Sherman, Texas, race with a speed of 420.730 miles per hour. For Reno 1990, piloting duties had been taken over by Skip Holm, who qualified *Tsunami* at 465.2 miles per hour and finished second in the Gold Championship at a blistering 462.999 miles per hour, pushing winner Lyle Shelton every inch of the way. For Reno 1991, Holm qualified second at 456.908 miles per hour and finished the Gold Championship in third at 478.140 miles per hour. However, disaster struck on 25 September as John Sandberg was flying *Tsunami* back to his home base in Minnesota. The racer was on final to Pierre, South Dakota, for a refueling stop, but when the flaps were lowered, only the right flap deployed. The racer rolled upside down and impacted the ground, killing Sandberg instantly and thus ending the career of one of the most promising of all racing aircraft.

Dave Cornell are nearing completion of an R-3350–powered racer that uses components from a Navy T-2 Buckeye jet trainer; famed air racer Darryl Greenamyer is proceeding with *Shock Wave*, a new-built racer using Sea Fury outer wing panels for its main wings and a tail from an F-86 Sabre; the remains of the highly modified Yak-11 *Mr. Awesome* have been resurrected into a new racer—and so it goes. Man's quest for speed in the air goes back to the earliest days of powered flight, and it is a quest that is only limited by human creativity and skill.

One of the strangest Unlimited racing creations was started in the late 1970s at Van Nuys Airport in southern California. Using the frame of a North American T-6 Texan, several partners hoped to create "the world's fastest aircraft." Whoever was doing the advising was, at best, ill-advised. The completed creation, named *Wildfire*, is seen at Mojave Airport during June 1983. Power was provided by a Pratt & Whitney R-2800 with a four-bladed propeller and spinner, and a huge slab wing was specially built for the project. Brave test pilot Joe Guthrie took the aircraft aloft in 1983 for its one and only flight. Apparently, the center of gravity was completely out of whack, and Guthrie had to do everything in his power to keep the wildly bucking racer under control. Somehow, he managed to pull off a successful landing and walked away from the craft—never looking back. Since then, *Wildfire* has remained firmly locked in a Mojave hangar.

Perhaps the most costly and least successful of modern Unlimited racing aircraft, the Pond Racer is seen at its unveiling at Mojave, California, on 4 April 1991. Designed and built by Burt Rutan at his Mojave facility, the Pond Racer was radical in appearance, with twin engines, and a center pod for the pilot highly modified automotive. The theory behind the Pond Racer was that the small size of the aircraft coupled with the high-tech racing engines (capable of producing 1,000 horsepower each) would produce an aircraft that could race in the region of 500 miles per hour. The pilot would be isolated from the engines and fuel, thus, according to Rutan, offering a much safer position. The twin powerplants, Electromotive Nissan V-6 racing engines, were built to run on either aviation gas or a custom alcohol fuel (at race power, the alcohol fuel would only last for 20 minutes). With both the Electromotive powerplants running, the Pond Racer heads for a test flight at Mojave. The pilot chosen to fly the Pond Racer at Reno was Rick Brickert. The Pond Racer crew stated that Reno 1991 would be more of an experience-gathering race than an all-out competitive event for the new plane. Even so, Brickert qualified the craft at 400 miles per hour, even though the engines were apparently only putting out around 600 horsepower each. From that point on, the Pond Racer had nothing but problems—starting all three of its assigned heat races but completing only a total of five laps because engine problems plagued the craft. The Pond Racer never lived up to its design specifications, and the closest it ever came to a victory was a second place in the 1992 Bronze race, coming in behind a stock Mustang. At Reno 1993, Rick Brickert, one of the most popular of all race pilots, died in the crash of the Pond Racer. It appears that the aircraft had at least one engine out when it impacted near the field, but the cause of the accident remains unexplained.

American warbird collectors are always on the lookout for vintage aircraft, so when a large cache of ex-Egyptian Air Force Yakovlev Yak-11 two-seat advanced trainers became available, numerous examples were imported and several were converted for air racing. The attractive Yak, the design of which was based on the successful World War II Yak-3 fighter series, was built by several communist countries, and an estimated 4,500 examples were constructed. Originally powered by an ASh-21 radial of around 750 horsepower, racing Yaks have had American engines of various types installed. One of the most successful Yak modifications was the Yak-11 flown by Bob Yancey. Race number 101 featured extensive modifications, including a metalized fuselage with a low drag canopy, American systems, and a powerful R-2800 mounted up front. With over 2,000 available horsepower, Yancey's Yak-11 first appeared at Reno 1988 and immediately began turning high lap speeds. Each year, barring mechanical problems, the Yak increased its speed into the mid-400s, amazing performance for what had been a training aircraft. Bob Yancey decided to retire from air racing, so in late 1995, race number 101 was sold to Alan Preston, who plans to add a few more aerodynamic modifications.

During the early 1990s, race pilot Alan Preston struck a deal with the Yakovlev factory in Russia to begin producing Yak-3 fighters where they had left off in 1945! Built to original plans and specifications, the aircraft were fitted with Allison V-1710 V-12 engines because the original Soviet engines were no longer available. The "new" World War II fighters began arriving in the United States in 1993, and Preston entered NX494DJ, race number 12, at Reno 1994 where it came in second, with no race modifications, in the Bronze race with Bruce Lockwood at the controls. Seen over Mojave on 19 May, race number 12 is being flown by Steve Hinton. As this book was going to press, Preston was planning an all-Yak racing team with three aircraft suitably modified for the Bronze, Silver, and Gold events.

Only a few pilots could do this (note the angle of attack): Famed race pilot Skip Holm flies formation in the most wild of all modified Yaks—Joe Kasparoff's R-3350-powered racer—with Jack Ward flying the T-6 Texan camera plane at full power in a slight dive. This photograph from August 1988 shows Kasparoff's Yak on its fourth test flight. Designed and built by the talented group of air-race enthusiasts that call Van Nuys Airport home, most of the original fuselage was redesigned and reconstructed with much larger and stronger tubing to take the power of the Wright radial, which was equipped with Power Recovery Turbines (PRTs), making its perhaps the ultimate piston engine, one capable of 3,700 horsepower. The massive engine is supported by the stock Yak-11 wing, and the lengthened fuselage is clearly visible. The stock tail is also apparent, and this unit immediately caused stability problems.

For Reno 1989, *Mr. Awesome*, ownership of which had transferred to Darryl Greenamyer, had received some heavy-duty modifications in order to improve stability. The entire tail unit of a Lockheed T-33 had been grafted onto the racer, which is seen departing Van Nuys for Reno with Neil Anderson at the controls. After a wild takeoff, during which the tail wheel departed the racer, Anderson got *Mr. Awesome* stabilized and pressed on to Reno. Bad luck continued to plague the craft, and it was virtually destroyed in a crash landing after the engine failed. Fortunately, Anderson survived with just some bruises. The remains of the plane were sold to another pilot, who as we go to press was preparing to test fly a resurrected *Mr. Awesome*.

Index